Accounting Ledger Book

Name:	Position:
Adress:	
Mobile:	
Telephone:	
Email:	
Fax:	

Book info :

Book No.:	Continued from book No.:
Start Date:	End Date:

Notes:

_____

_____

_____

_____

_____

_____

ACCOUNTING LEDGER

PAGE.No.

Account Name And Number :

Year : _____   Month : _____

No.	Date	Description	Account	Reference	Debit	−	Credit	+	Total

ACCOUNTING LEDGER

PAGE.No.

Account Name And Number :

Year : _____   Month : _____

No.	Date	Description	Account	Reference	Debit	—	Credit	+	Total

ACCOUNTING LEDGER

PAGE.No.

Account Name And Number :

Year : _____   Month : _____

No.	Date	Description	Account	Reference	Debit	−	Credit	+	Total

ACCOUNTING LEDGER

PAGE.No.

Account Name And Number :

Year : _____   **Month : _____**

No.	Date	Description	Account	Reference	Debit	−	Credit	+	Total

ACCOUNTING LEDGER

Account Name And Number :

Year : _____   Month : _____

No.	Date	Description	Account	Reference	Debit	−	Credit	+	Total

ACCOUNTING LEDGER

PAGE.No.

Account Name And Number :

Year : _____   **Month :** _____

No.	Date	Description	Account	Reference	Debit	−	Credit	+	Total

ACCOUNTING LEDGER

PAGE.No.

Account Name And Number :

Year : _____   Month : _____

No.	Date	Description	Account	Reference	Debit	−	Credit	+	Total

ACCOUNTING LEDGER

PAGE.No.

Account Name And Number :

Year : _____   Month : _____

No.	Date	Description	Account	Reference	Debit	−	Credit	+	Total

ACCOUNTING LEDGER

PAGE.No.

Account Name And Number :

Year : _____   Month : _____

No.	Date	Description	Account	Reference	Debit	−	Credit	+	Total

ACCOUNTING LEDGER

PAGE.No.

Account Name And Number :

Year : _____   **Month :** _____

No.	Date	Description	Account	Reference	Debit	−	Credit	+	Total

ACCOUNTING LEDGER

PAGE.No.

Account Name And Number :

Year : _____   Month : _____

No.	Date	Description	Account	Reference	Debit	−	Credit	+	Total

ACCOUNTING LEDGER

PAGE.No.

Account Name And Number :

Year : _____   Month : _____

No.	Date	Description	Account	Reference	Debit	−	Credit	+	Total

ACCOUNTING LEDGER

PAGE.No.

Account Name And Number :

Year : _____   **Month : _____**

No.	Date	Description	Account	Reference	Debit	−	Credit	+	Total

ACCOUNTING LEDGER

PAGE.No. _____

Account Name And Number : _____

Year : _____   **Month :** _____

No.	Date	Description	Account	Reference	Debit	—	Credit	+	Total

ACCOUNTING LEDGER

PAGE.No.

Account Name And Number :

Year : _____   Month : _____

No.	Date	Description	Account	Reference	Debit	−	Credit	+	Total

ACCOUNTING LEDGER

PAGE.No.

Account Name And Number :

Year : _____   Month : _____

No.	Date	Description	Account	Reference	Debit	−	Credit	+	Total

ACCOUNTING LEDGER

PAGE.No.

Account Name And Number :

Year : _____   **Month : _____**

No.	Date	Description	Account	Reference	Debit	−	Credit	+	Total

ACCOUNTING LEDGER

PAGE.No.

Account Name And Number :

Year : _____

Month : _____

No.	Date	Description	Account	Reference	Debit	−	Credit	+	Total

ACCOUNTING LEDGER

Account Name And Number :

Year : _____   **Month : _____**

No.	Date	Description	Account	Reference	Debit	−	Credit	+	Total

ACCOUNTING LEDGER

PAGE.No.

Account Name And Number :

Year : _____   **Month :** _____

No.	Date	Description	Account	Reference	Debit	−	Credit	+	Total

ACCOUNTING LEDGER

PAGE.No.

Account Name And Number :

Year : _____   Month : _____

No.	Date	Description	Account	Reference	Debit	−	Credit	+	Total

ACCOUNTING LEDGER

PAGE.No.

Account Name And Number :

Year : _____　　　　　　　　　　　　　**Month : _____**

No.	Date	Description	Account	Reference	Debit	−	Credit	+	Total

ACCOUNTING LEDGER

PAGE.No.

Account Name And Number :

Year : _____   Month : _____

No.	Date	Description	Account	Reference	Debit	−	Credit	+	Total

ACCOUNTING LEDGER

PAGE.No.

Account Name And Number :

Year : _____   **Month : _____**

No.	Date	Description	Account	Reference	Debit	−	Credit	+	Total

ACCOUNTING LEDGER

PAGE.No.

Account Name And Number :

Year : _____   Month : _____

No.	Date	Description	Account	Reference	Debit	−	Credit	+	Total

ACCOUNTING LEDGER

PAGE.No.

Account Name And Number :

Year : _____

Month : _____

No.	Date	Description	Account	Reference	Debit	—	Credit	+	Total

ACCOUNTING LEDGER

PAGE.No.

Account Name And Number :

Year : _____   Month : _____

No.	Date	Description	Account	Reference	Debit	−	Credit	+	Total

ACCOUNTING LEDGER

PAGE.No.

Account Name And Number :

Year : _____

Month : _____

No.	Date	Description	Account	Reference	Debit	−	Credit	+	Total

ACCOUNTING LEDGER

PAGE.No.

Account Name And Number :

Year : _____   **Month : _____**

No.	Date	Description	Account	Reference	Debit	−	Credit	+	Total

ACCOUNTING LEDGER

PAGE.No.

Account Name And Number :

Year : _____

Month : _____

No.	Date	Description	Account	Reference	Debit	−	Credit	+	Total

ACCOUNTING LEDGER

PAGE.No.

Account Name And Number :

Year : _____   Month : _____

No.	Date	Description	Account	Reference	Debit	−	Credit	+	Total

ACCOUNTING LEDGER

PAGE.No.

Account Name And Number :

Year : _____   Month : _____

No.	Date	Description	Account	Reference	Debit	−	Credit	+	Total

ACCOUNTING LEDGER

PAGE.No.

Account Name And Number :

Year : _____   Month : _____

No.	Date	Description	Account	Reference	Debit	−	Credit	+	Total

ACCOUNTING LEDGER

PAGE.No.

Account Name And Number :

Year : _____   Month : _____

No.	Date	Description	Account	Reference	Debit	−	Credit	+	Total

ACCOUNTING LEDGER

PAGE.No.

Account Name And Number :

Year : _____   Month : _____

No.	Date	Description	Account	Reference	Debit	−	Credit	+	Total

ACCOUNTING LEDGER

PAGE.No.

Account Name And Number :

Year : _____ Month : _____

No.	Date	Description	Account	Reference	Debit	−	Credit	+	Total

ACCOUNTING LEDGER

PAGE.No.

Account Name And Number :

Year : _____ Month : _____

No.	Date	Description	Account	Reference	Debit	−	Credit	+	Total

ACCOUNTING LEDGER

PAGE.No.

Account Name And Number :

Year : _____   Month : _____

No.	Date	Description	Account	Reference	Debit	−	Credit	+	Total

ACCOUNTING LEDGER

PAGE.No.

Account Name And Number :

Year : _____   Month : _____

No.	Date	Description	Account	Reference	Debit	−	Credit	+	Total

ACCOUNTING LEDGER

PAGE.No.

Account Name And Number :

Year : _____   **Month :** _____

No.	Date	Description	Account	Reference	Debit	−	Credit	+	Total

ACCOUNTING LEDGER

PAGE.No.

Account Name And Number :

Year : _____   Month : _____

No.	Date	Description	Account	Reference	Debit	−	Credit	+	Total

ACCOUNTING LEDGER

PAGE.No.

Account Name And Number :

Year : _____   **Month :** _____

No.	Date	Description	Account	Reference	Debit	−	Credit	+	Total

ACCOUNTING LEDGER

PAGE.No.

Account Name And Number :

Year : _____   Month : _____

No.	Date	Description	Account	Reference	Debit	−	Credit	+	Total

ACCOUNTING LEDGER

PAGE.No.

Account Name And Number :

Year : _____   Month : _____

No.	Date	Description	Account	Reference	Debit	−	Credit	+	Total

ACCOUNTING LEDGER

PAGE.No.

Account Name And Number :

Year : _____   Month : _____

No.	Date	Description	Account	Reference	Debit	—	Credit	+	Total

ACCOUNTING LEDGER

PAGE.No.

Account Name And Number :

Year : _____

Month : _____

No.	Date	Description	Account	Reference	Debit	−	Credit	+	Total

ACCOUNTING LEDGER

PAGE.No.

Account Name And Number :

Year : _____ Month : _____

No.	Date	Description	Account	Reference	Debit	−	Credit	+	Total

ACCOUNTING LEDGER

PAGE.No.

Account Name And Number :

Year : _____   Month : _____

No.	Date	Description	Account	Reference	Debit	—	Credit	+	Total

ACCOUNTING LEDGER

PAGE.No.

Account Name And Number :

Year : _____   Month : _____

No.	Date	Description	Account	Reference	Debit	−	Credit	+	Total

ACCOUNTING LEDGER

PAGE.No.

Account Name And Number :

Year : _____   Month : _____

No.	Date	Description	Account	Reference	Debit	−	Credit	+	Total

ACCOUNTING LEDGER

PAGE.No.

Account Name And Number :

Year : _____   **Month : _____**

No.	Date	Description	Account	Reference	Debit	−	Credit	+	Total

ACCOUNTING LEDGER

PAGE.No.

Account Name And Number :

Year : _____   Month : _____

No.	Date	Description	Account	Reference	Debit	—	Credit	+	Total

ACCOUNTING LEDGER

PAGE.No.

Account Name And Number :

Year : _____   **Month : _____**

No.	Date	Description	Account	Reference	Debit	−	Credit	+	Total

ACCOUNTING LEDGER

PAGE.No.

Account Name And Number :

Year : _____   Month : _____

No.	Date	Description	Account	Reference	Debit	—	Credit	+	Total

ACCOUNTING LEDGER

PAGE.No.

Account Name And Number :

Year : _____   Month : _____

No.	Date	Description	Account	Reference	Debit	−	Credit	+	Total

ACCOUNTING LEDGER

PAGE.No.

Account Name And Number :

Year : _____   Month : _____

No.	Date	Description	Account	Reference	Debit	—	Credit	+	Total

ACCOUNTING LEDGER

PAGE.No.

Account Name And Number :

Year : _____   Month : _____

No.	Date	Description	Account	Reference	Debit	−	Credit	+	Total

ACCOUNTING LEDGER

PAGE.No.

Account Name And Number :

Year : _____   **Month : _____**

No.	Date	Description	Account	Reference	Debit	−	Credit	+	Total

ACCOUNTING LEDGER

PAGE.No.

Account Name And Number :

Year : _____   Month : _____

No.	Date	Description	Account	Reference	Debit	—	Credit	+	Total

ACCOUNTING LEDGER

PAGE.No.

Account Name And Number :

Year : _____　　　　　　　　　　　　　　**Month : _____**

No.	Date	Description	Account	Reference	Debit	−	Credit	+	Total

ACCOUNTING LEDGER

PAGE.No.

Account Name And Number :

Year : _____   Month : _____

No.	Date	Description	Account	Reference	Debit	−	Credit	+	Total

ACCOUNTING LEDGER

PAGE.No.

Account Name And Number :

Year : _____   **Month :** _____

No.	Date	Description	Account	Reference	Debit	—	Credit	+	Total

ACCOUNTING LEDGER

PAGE.No.

Account Name And Number :

Year : _____ **Month : _____**

No.	Date	Description	Account	Reference	Debit	−	Credit	+	Total

ACCOUNTING LEDGER

PAGE.No.

Account Name And Number :

Year : ＿＿＿＿   Month : ＿＿＿＿

No.	Date	Description	Account	Reference	Debit	—	Credit	+	Total

ACCOUNTING LEDGER

PAGE.No.

Account Name And Number :

Year : _____   Month : _____

No.	Date	Description	Account	Reference	Debit	−	Credit	+	Total

ACCOUNTING LEDGER

PAGE.No.

Account Name And Number :

Year : ____

Month : ____

No.	Date	Description	Account	Reference	Debit	−	Credit	+	Total

ACCOUNTING LEDGER

PAGE.No.

Account Name And Number :

Year : _____   Month : _____

No.	Date	Description	Account	Reference	Debit	−	Credit	+	Total

ACCOUNTING LEDGER

PAGE.No.

Account Name And Number :

Year : _____

Month : _____

No.	Date	Description	Account	Reference	Debit	−	Credit	+	Total

ACCOUNTING LEDGER

Account Name And Number :

Year : _____   Month : _____

No.	Date	Description	Account	Reference	Debit	−	Credit	+	Total

ACCOUNTING LEDGER

PAGE.No.

Account Name And Number :

Year : _____   **Month :** _____

No.	Date	Description	Account	Reference	Debit	−	Credit	+	Total

ACCOUNTING LEDGER

PAGE.No.

Account Name And Number :

Year : _____   Month : _____

No.	Date	Description	Account	Reference	Debit	−	Credit	+	Total

ACCOUNTING LEDGER

PAGE.No.

Account Name And Number :

Year : _____   Month : _____

No.	Date	Description	Account	Reference	Debit	−	Credit	+	Total

ACCOUNTING LEDGER

PAGE.No.

Account Name And Number :

Year : _____   Month : _____

No.	Date	Description	Account	Reference	Debit	−	Credit	+	Total

ACCOUNTING LEDGER

PAGE.No. ____

Account Name And Number : ____

Year : ____   **Month :** ____

No.	Date	Description	Account	Reference	Debit	−	Credit	+	Total

ACCOUNTING LEDGER

PAGE.No.

Account Name And Number :

Year : _____   Month : _____

No.	Date	Description	Account	Reference	Debit	—	Credit	+	Total

ACCOUNTING LEDGER

PAGE.No.

Account Name And Number :

Year : _____   **Month :** _____

No.	Date	Description	Account	Reference	Debit	−	Credit	+	Total

ACCOUNTING LEDGER

PAGE.No.

Account Name And Number :

Year : _____   Month : _____

No.	Date	Description	Account	Reference	Debit	−	Credit	+	Total

ACCOUNTING LEDGER

PAGE.No.

Account Name And Number :

Year : _____   **Month :** _____

No.	Date	Description	Account	Reference	Debit	−	Credit	+	Total

ACCOUNTING LEDGER

PAGE.No.

Account Name And Number :

Year : _____   Month : _____

No.	Date	Description	Account	Reference	Debit	—	Credit	+	Total

ACCOUNTING LEDGER

PAGE.No.

Account Name And Number :

Year : _____   **Month :** _____

No.	Date	Description	Account	Reference	Debit	—	Credit	+	Total

ACCOUNTING LEDGER

PAGE.No.

Account Name And Number :

Year : _____   Month : _____

No.	Date	Description	Account	Reference	Debit	−	Credit	+	Total

ACCOUNTING LEDGER

PAGE.No.

Account Name And Number :

Year : _____   **Month :** _____

No.	Date	Description	Account	Reference	Debit	−	Credit	+	Total

ACCOUNTING LEDGER

PAGE.No.

Account Name And Number :

Year : _____   Month : _____

No.	Date	Description	Account	Reference	Debit	−	Credit	+	Total

ACCOUNTING LEDGER

PAGE.No. ___

Account Name And Number : ___

Year : ____ **Month :** ____

No.	Date	Description	Account	Reference	Debit	−	Credit	+	Total

ACCOUNTING LEDGER

PAGE.No.

Account Name And Number :

Year : _____   Month : _____

No.	Date	Description	Account	Reference	Debit	−	Credit	+	Total

ACCOUNTING LEDGER

PAGE.No.

Account Name And Number :

Year : _____   **Month :** _____

No.	Date	Description	Account	Reference	Debit	−	Credit	+	Total

ACCOUNTING LEDGER

PAGE.No.

Account Name And Number :

Year : _____   **Month : _____**

No.	Date	Description	Account	Reference	Debit	−	Credit	+	Total

ACCOUNTING LEDGER

PAGE.No.

Account Name And Number :

Year : _____   **Month :** _____

No.	Date	Description	Account	Reference	Debit	−	Credit	+	Total

ACCOUNTING LEDGER

PAGE.No.

Account Name And Number :

Year : _____   **Month :** _____

No.	Date	Description	Account	Reference	Debit	−	Credit	+	Total

ACCOUNTING LEDGER

PAGE.No.

Account Name And Number :

Year : _____

Month : _____

No.	Date	Description	Account	Reference	Debit	−	Credit	+	Total

ACCOUNTING LEDGER

PAGE.No.

Account Name And Number :

Year : ____   Month : ____

No.	Date	Description	Account	Reference	Debit	−	Credit	+	Total

ACCOUNTING LEDGER

PAGE.No.

Account Name And Number :

Year : ____   **Month :** ____

No.	Date	Description	Account	Reference	Debit	−	Credit	+	Total

ACCOUNTING LEDGER

PAGE.No.

Account Name And Number :

Year : _____   **Month : _____**

No.	Date	Description	Account	Reference	Debit	−	Credit	+	Total

ACCOUNTING LEDGER

PAGE.No.

Account Name And Number :

Year : _____   **Month :** _____

No.	Date	Description	Account	Reference	Debit	−	Credit	+	Total

ACCOUNTING LEDGER

PAGE.No.

Account Name And Number :

Year : _____   Month : _____

No.	Date	Description	Account	Reference	Debit	−	Credit	+	Total

ACCOUNTING LEDGER

PAGE.No.

Account Name And Number :

Year : ____   **Month :** _____

No.	Date	Description	Account	Reference	Debit	—	Credit	+	Total

ACCOUNTING LEDGER

PAGE.No.

Account Name And Number :

Year : _____   Month : _____

No.	Date	Description	Account	Reference	Debit	−	Credit	+	Total

ACCOUNTING LEDGER

PAGE.No.

Account Name And Number :

Year : _____   **Month :** _____

No.	Date	Description	Account	Reference	Debit	−	Credit	+	Total

ACCOUNTING LEDGER

PAGE.No.

Account Name And Number :

Year : _____   **Month : _____**

No.	Date	Description	Account	Reference	Debit	−	Credit	+	Total

ACCOUNTING LEDGER

PAGE.No.

Account Name And Number :

Year : _____   **Month :** _____

No.	Date	Description	Account	Reference	Debit	−	Credit	+	Total

ACCOUNTING LEDGER

PAGE.No.

Account Name And Number :

Year : _____   Month : _____

No.	Date	Description	Account	Reference	Debit	−	Credit	+	Total

ACCOUNTING LEDGER

PAGE.No.

Account Name And Number :

Year : _____   **Month :** _____

No.	Date	Description	Account	Reference	Debit	−	Credit	+	Total

ACCOUNTING LEDGER

PAGE.No.

Account Name And Number :

Year : _____   Month : _____

No.	Date	Description	Account	Reference	Debit	−	Credit	+	Total

ACCOUNTING LEDGER

PAGE.No.

Account Name And Number :

Year : _____ **Month : _____**

No.	Date	Description	Account	Reference	Debit	−	Credit	+	Total

ACCOUNTING LEDGER

PAGE.No.

Account Name And Number :

Year : _____   Month : _____

No.	Date	Description	Account	Reference	Debit	−	Credit	+	Total

ACCOUNTING LEDGER

PAGE.No.

Account Name And Number :

Year : _____　　　　　　　　　　　　**Month : _____**

No.	Date	Description	Account	Reference	Debit	−	Credit	+	Total

ACCOUNTING LEDGER

PAGE.No.

Account Name And Number :

Year : _____   Month : _____

No.	Date	Description	Account	Reference	Debit	−	Credit	+	Total

ACCOUNTING LEDGER

PAGE.No.

Account Name And Number :

Year : _____   **Month :** _____

No.	Date	Description	Account	Reference	Debit	−	Credit	+	Total

ACCOUNTING LEDGER

PAGE.No.

Account Name And Number :

Year : _____   **Month : _____**

No.	Date	Description	Account	Reference	Debit	−	Credit	+	Total

ACCOUNTING LEDGER

PAGE.No.

Account Name And Number :

Year : _____   **Month :** _____

No.	Date	Description	Account	Reference	Debit	−	Credit	+	Total

ACCOUNTING LEDGER

PAGE.No.

Account Name And Number :

Year : _____   Month : _____

No.	Date	Description	Account	Reference	Debit	−	Credit	+	Total

ACCOUNTING LEDGER

PAGE.No.

Account Name And Number :

Year : _____   Month : _____

No.	Date	Description	Account	Reference	Debit	−	Credit	+	Total

Thank you!

WE ARE GLAD THAT YOU PURCHASED OUR BOOK!
PLEASE LET US KNOW HOW WE CAN IMPROVE IT!
YOUR FEEDBACK IS ESSENTIAL TO US.

Contact us at:

M log'Sin@gmail.com

___

JUST TITLE THE EMAIL 'CREATIVE' AND WE WILL

GIVE YOU SOME EXTRA SURPRISES!

www.ingramcontent.com/pod-product-compliance
Lightning Source LLC
Chambersburg PA
CBHW051758200326

41597CB00025B/4603